LOS ANGELES 2013

THE CITY AT A GLANCE

C000163071

777 Tower

Pelli Clarke Pelli's 52-storey white-
and-glass tower, completed in 1990
about distinctive enough to stand
the crowded Downtown skyline.
777 S Figueroa Street

Millennium Biltmore Hotel

Opened in 1923, this is one of LA's oldest
hotels. It warrants a visit if only to see
the ornate Italian-Spanish renaissance-
style architectural touches first hand.
506 S Grand Avenue, T 213 624 1011

US Bank Tower

The tallest structure in California has also
become Los Angeles' defining skyscraper.
Designed by Henry N Cobb and finished in
1989, the 310m tower can also boast the
world's highest rooftop helipad.
633 W 5th Street

Cathedral of Saint Vibiana

This vast complex became Los Angeles'
cathedral on completion in 1876. One of the
last remnants of 19th-century architecture
in the city, it now functions as an events space.
214 S Main Street

Caltrans District 7 Headquarters

For some, this building suggested the aliens
had landed but, for the Pritzker jury, Thom
Mayne's Department of Transportation HQ
represented the rootless nature of the city.
See p010

Walt Disney Concert Hall

Buried among the Downtown skyscrapers,
Frank Gehry's home for the Los Angeles
Philharmonic, finished in 2003, is an
absolute must-see, both inside and out.
See p014

INTRODUCTION
THE CHANGING FACE OF THE URBAN SCENE

It's long been easy to knock LA. Even Raymond Chandler, the city's laureate, called it a 'big hard-boiled city, with no more personality than a paper cup', lambasting the 'drab anonymity of a thousand shabby lives' lived out there – and that was in the good times. Well, things have changed and, more than a decade into the 21st century, LA is holding its own as a lure for commercial and cultural heavy hitters. Tourism shows no sign of slowing and the hospitality and retail industries are thriving, in spite of the economic crunch.

This refound confidence is visible in the string of design-led eateries, bars and hotels that pepper the city, especially in the high-priced arc running from the hip W Hollywood (6250 Hollywood Boulevard, T 323 798 1300) to the Shangri-La (see p020) in more sedate but newly buzzy Santa Monica. Revived neighbourhood Silver Lake has become a hot residential and retail address, and Culver City now attracts upmarket companies, restaurants and galleries. Further out, Eagle Rock and Glendale are also gentrifying fast. Meanwhile, Downtown and its nightlife continue to flourish.

The city of Eames, Neutra and 'Googie' has had few equals in its affection for challenging architecture and interiors, and it shows in the rows of stores still stocking midcentury modern sideboards, and the star status given to the people creating the look of today's LA. The city remains a bellwether for the kind of high-end design that, one day, will be the backdrop to all our leisure hours.

ESSENTIAL INFO
FACTS, FIGURES AND USEFUL ADDRESSES

TOURIST OFFICE
Hollywood & Highland Center
6801 Hollywood Boulevard
T 323 467 6412
www.discoverlosangeles.com

TRANSPORT
Car hire
Avis
T 213 533 8400
Hertz
T 213 625 1034
Metro (buses and trains)
T 213 922 6000
www.metro.net
Trains run from roughly 4am to 12am daily
Taxis
Independent Cab Co
T 310 521 8294
Yellow Cab
T 310 808 1000
It's advisable to order a cab in advance

EMERGENCY SERVICES
Emergencies
T 911
Police (non-emergencies)
Central Community Police Station
251 E 6th Street
T 213 485 3294
24-hour pharmacy
CVS
2530 Glendale Boulevard
T 323 666 1285
www.cvs.com

CONSULATE
British Consulate
Suite 1200
11766 Wilshire Boulevard
T 310 481 0031
www.ukinusa.fco.gov.uk

POSTAL SERVICES
Post office
7101 S Central Avenue
T 800 275 8777
Shipping
UPS
3183 Wilshire Boulevard
T 323 939 6001

BOOKS
**Architecture of the Sun: Los Angeles
Modernism 1900-1970**
by Thomas S Hines (Rizzoli International)
LA 2000+ by John Leighton Chase
(Monacelli Press)

WEBSITES
Architecture/Design
www.aplusd.org
Art
www.moca.org
www.getty.edu
Newspapers
www.latimes.com

EVENTS
Art Los Angeles Contemporary
www.artlosangelesfair.com
Los Angeles Design Festival
www.ladesignfestival.org

COST OF LIVING
Taxi from LAX Airport to Hollywood
$70
Cappuccino
$3.50
Packet of cigarettes
$5
Daily newspaper
$1
Bottle of champagne
$100

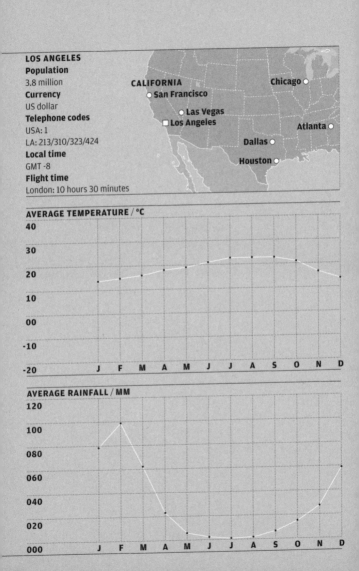

LOS ANGELES
Population
3.8 million
Currency
US dollar
Telephone codes
USA: 1
LA: 213/310/323/424
Local time
GMT -8
Flight time
London: 10 hours 30 minutes

CALIFORNIA
San Francisco
Las Vegas
Los Angeles
Chicago
Atlanta
Dallas
Houston

AVERAGE TEMPERATURE / °C

40
30
20
10
00
-10
-20

J F M A M J J A S O N D

AVERAGE RAINFALL / MM

120
100
080
060
040
020
000

J F M A M J J A S O N D

NEIGHBOURHOODS

THE AREAS YOU NEED TO KNOW AND WHY

To help you navigate the city, we've chosen the most interesting districts (see below and the map inside the back cover) and colour-coded our featured venues, according to their location; those venues that are outside these areas are not coloured.

WEST HOLLYWOOD/MIDTOWN

A contender for the heart of the western side of the city, WeHo is home to LA's gay district and, not coincidentally, some of its most sumptuous designer shopping, on tiny Melrose Place. There are plenty of places to eat and be seen, in addition to an ever-growing list of hip hotels, such as the Andaz (see p021) and, of course, the unmissable Chateau Marmont (see p028).

SANTA MONICA/VENICE/CULVER CITY

Santa Monica has always been affluent, but a few overhauls in recent years – such as the revamped Hotel Shangri-La (see p020) and Annenberg Community Beach House (see p092) – have given it a new edge. Abbot Kinney Boulevard in artsy Venice has long been rattling to the sound of the gentrifiers' hammers, while Culver City's influx of galleries, media companies and interesting architecture, including Samitaur Tower (see p065), have made this 'burb worth a visit.

HOLLYWOOD

Although it may be awash with tourist tat, Hollywood Boulevard's side streets are home to cool bars like The Parlour Room (see p048), and several high-calibre restaurants. The Hollywood and Vine intersection is the focal point, where hot venues, such as Katsuya (6300 Hollywood Boulevard, T 323 871 8777), have been opening faster than you can scatter the pins at The Spare Room (see p038).

LOS FELIZ/SILVER LAKE/ECHO PARK

Largely residential, with houses designed by Richard Neutra, Rudolph Schindler and Frank Lloyd Wright (see p064), Silver Lake is also full of shops such as Clare Vivier's eponymous bag store (3339 W Sunset Boulevard, T 323 665 2476), and cafés like Lamill Coffee (see p049). Dine at Mess Hall (4500 Los Feliz Boulevard, T 323 660 6377) or Black Hogg (see p053).

BEVERLY HILLS/WESTWOOD

Until recently, this old-money 'hood lacked panache, but chic hotels like the Thompson (9360 Wilshire Boulevard, T 310 273 1400) and eateries such as Bouchon (235 N Canon Drive, T 310 271 9910) changed that. It also retains industry magic in hidden places; check out the Fountain Coffee Room at The Beverly Hills Hotel (9641 Sunset Boulevard, T 310 276 2251) for a latte with the movie moguls. Westwood is the home of Richard Meier's Getty Center (T 310 440 7300), with its superb views over LA.

DOWNTOWN

There was a time when there was little to lure anyone here and, after hours, the only people you'd come across would be the homeless. Thanks to entertainment hub LA Live (800 W Olympic Boulevard, T 866 548 3452) and a rush of fabulous eateries, from WP24 (see p059) to Bottega Louie (700 S Grand Avenue, T 213 802 1470), Downtown has certainly arrived. Don't miss the Walt Disney Concert Hall (see p014).

LANDMARKS
THE SHAPE OF THE CITY SKYLINE

Some of the most acclaimed film treatments of LA, from *Short Cuts* and *Pulp Fiction* to *Magnolia* and *Crash*, have been narratives that capture the city using multiple, interwoven storylines. They echo the alienating sprawl of this megalopolis and reveal its potential to put the fear of God into first-time visitors. In fact, thanks to the mountains to the north, ocean to the west and its well-signposted boulevards and freeways, LA is surprisingly easy to navigate.

But you must, must have a car. The main areas to explore lie along a curve sweeping north-west from Downtown, through Hollywood to Venice. Latino East LA and the San Fernando Valley to the north have pockets of interest, but the visitor is unlikely to have enough time to seek them out. Instead, head to Silver Lake for SoCal (Southern Californian) architecture and Downtown for more contemporary pleasures, such as MOCA (250 S Grand Avenue, T 213 626 6222), the Caltrans HQ (overleaf) and Frank Gehry's Walt Disney Concert Hall (see p014). Up in north-east Hollywood is the Hollywood Seventh-Day Adventist Church (1711 N Van Ness Avenue, T 323 462 0010), a true LA landmark in that it sits at the Hollywood Freeway/Hollywood Boulevard intersection and is passed by thousands of drivers each day. Its curved concrete form has been described as a 'boat of faith, riding on a sea of humanity' or, more prosaically, as 'God's own gas station'.
For full addresses, see Resources.

Caltrans District 7 Headquarters

This is the building that helped Thom Mayne bring the Pritzker Prize back to America in 2005, for the first time in 14 years. Likened by some detractors to the Death Star, the Caltrans HQ certainly is imposing – a matt grey metal hulk of a building that takes up a whole city block – but it is made graceful by the many perforations in its panelled aluminium skin, the folds and openings of which break up the structure's lines. Keith Sonnier's neon installation, *Motordom*, suggestive of brake lights on an LA freeway, adds some much-needed levity. If you stand on the north-west corner of the junction of Broadway and First Street, you can see the Walt Disney Concert Hall (see p014) and the Caltrans HQ at the same time.
100 S Main Street

Norms Restaurant
Everyone has their favourite 'Googie', a nickname given to a style of modern architecture introduced by John Lautner in 1949. Pann's in Inglewood (T 310 670 1441) is often cited as the best example, but it's not exactly central. Norms is in the heart of West Hollywood and doesn't feel like a tourist attraction or an architecture museum. It's a living structure, a little shabby at the edges and in need of some new ceiling tiles, but worth a visit for its space-age lampshades alone. It's also a handy place to while away a few hours, drink endless cups of coffee and chat to some down-to-earth locals at the lunch counter, should you tire of discussing Hans Wegner chairs around the corner in the La Cienega Design Quarter.
470 N La Cienega Boulevard, T 310 657 8333, www.normsrestaurants.com

Capitol Records Building

Drive south on the 101 Freeway into Hollywood and the first thing you'll see, through the smog, off the Vine Street exit, is Welton Becket & Associates' 1956 Capitol Records Building. Resembling a stack of discs, it was the world's first circular office building and is topped with a 'stylus needle' that blinks out 'Hollywood' in Morse code. Fittingly, you have to step over John Lennon's star on the Hollywood Walk of Fame to enter the gold-record-lined lobby. Capitol still has a working in-house recording studio here, where orchestras lay down tracks for the big awards shows. Knowing that The Beatles, The Beach Boys and Frank Sinatra have all walked through its doors makes this a landmark many times over.
1750 N Vine Street, T 323 871 5001, www.capitolrecords.com

Walt Disney Concert Hall
It has been described as a barge at full sail, a homage to the billowing skirts of Marilyn Monroe, a cubist masterpiece, and a physical manifestation of a certain cartoon mouse's strokes with his magic wand. It is, in fact, stunningly beautiful, universally lauded and a hometown stainless-steel victory for its designer, Frank Gehry. Some say it surpasses his Guggenheim Museum in Bilbao. Years of funding problems and delays almost killed the project, but following its opening in 2003, Gehry's building became the big, shiny hope of the city fathers, who prayed that it would bring some life back to the moribund Downtown area. If you get the chance, go to a concert (it's the home of the Los Angeles Philharmonic), if only to see the undulating form of the interior.
111 S Grand Avenue, T 323 850 2000, www.laphil.com

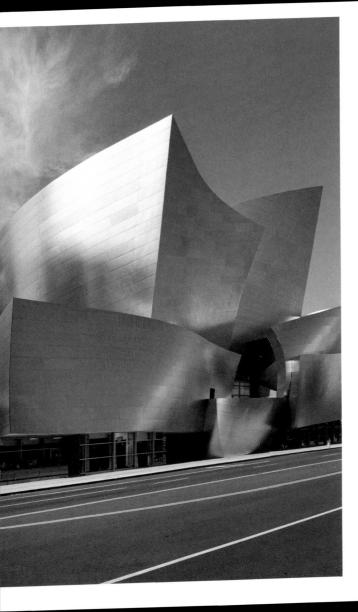

HOTELS

WHERE TO STAY AND WHICH ROOMS TO BOOK

LA has always been famous for its hotels, but the plethora of chic berths appearing in the past decade has revived its reputation for strong design. The people to thank for this include André Balazs, whose midcentury-meets-Gothic revamp of Chateau Marmont (see p028) has kept it at the top of the pile since the 1990s. Next, Balazs opened The Standard Hollywood (8300 Sunset Boulevard, T 323 650 9090) and The Standard Downtown (see p022), giving a sex-in-the-70s feel to an oil-company office block. Then came his chief rival, Kelly Wearstler, who took the old Beverly Carlton Hotel and carved out a modernist haven, the Avalon (see p026).

The latest wave is a mix of revamps and new properties that have injected a shot of contemporary luxe into the scene. Among the renovations is the 2011 transformation of the Hotel Bel-Air (opposite), while the SBE group followed its collaboration with Philippe Starck on the SLS Hotel (see p024) by working with Matthew Rolston on its takeover of The Redbury @ Hollywood and Vine (1717 Vine Street, T 323 962 1717). The long-stay 'urban lodges' at Palihouse (8465 Holloway Drive, T 323 656 4100) now have a short-term alternative in sister property Palihotel (7950 Melrose Avenue, T 323 272 4588). The 2013 opening of the Ace Hotel (929 S Broadway) in Downtown looks sure to cement the once scrappy district's arrival as a destination in its own right. *For full addresses and room rates, see Resources.*

Hotel Bel-Air

Originally opened in 1946, this Dorchester Collection property is almost as famous as the guests who made it their LA hideaway; Elizabeth Taylor was a regular and Grace Kelly slept here after winning her Oscar in 1955. It's since been revamped by interior designer Alexandra Champalimaud, who thankfully left the famous 'Bel-Air pink' exterior untouched, and was reopened in 2011. An updated lobby features limestone and naturally aged oak floors, and new accommodations include the Presidential Suite (above and overleaf), which has its own courtyard and pool. Luxury of a more affordable nature can be enjoyed here at Wolfgang Puck's eponymous restaurant (T 310 909 1644) and the 385 sq m Spa by La Prairie (T 310 909 1681). *701 Stone Canyon Road, T 310 472 1211, www.hotelbelair.com*

Presidential Suite, Hotel Bel-Air

Hotel Shangri-La

This landmark oceanside property in Santa Monica is an art deco gem. Owner Tamie Adaya liked it enough to spend a cool $30m restoring the place, which she, assisted by designer Marc Smith, did with aplomb. Many of the original 1930s features were retained and enhanced by modern elements such as Delia Cabral's jewel-toned, custom-made wallpaper. There are 70 rooms and suites, all with full or partial views of the ocean; the feel is akin to being on a luxury cruise liner, especially in the likes of the Rock'n'Roll Suite (above). The rooftop bar, Suite 700, has a particularly stunning vista – from here you can see from Catalina Island to the Hollywood Hills. The cabana-lined pool is a popular weekend hangout. *1301 Ocean Avenue, T 310 394 2791, www.shangrila-hotel.com*

Andaz West Hollywood

The hard-partying Hyatt, aka the 'Riot House', was an infamous hangout for bands such as Led Zeppelin and The Rolling Stones in the 1960s and 1970s; this is where Keith Richards hurled a TV from his 10th-floor room. Now, it's the sleek 239-room Andaz, designed by New York-based firm Janson Goldstein. The interiors meld modern furnishings with contemporary art, which includes Jacob Hashimoto's hand-painted metal sculpture in the lobby (above), fronting a glass pavilion and entrance to the well-reviewed RH bar/restaurant. Opt for one of the Sunset View King rooms facing Sunset Boulevard, which have glass sunrooms in place of the old balconies. The rooftop terrace is a great spot for a sundowner. *8401 Sunset Boulevard, T 323 656 1234, www.westhollywood.andaz.hyatt.com*

The Standard Downtown

This is *the* place to stay Downtown. It's camp, but in a good way, working it well in this macho former oil HQ. The design is by Koning Eizenberg Architecture, who created the fantastic all-night retro diner/restaurant; the Rooftop Bar, which set off a craze for high-altitude pool parties all over LA; and a stunning lobby (above). Guest rooms are fun and luxurious – the Huge Room, for example, has a tub opposite the bed and *The Man From UNCLE* fixtures and fittings. It seems that no opportunity for a double entendre has been passed up, judging by the pencils with 'Use Me' written on them, and room cards featuring the instruction 'Push Me In'. The risqué jokes do get stretched thin, however – perhaps more Austin Powers than Illya Kuryakin. *550 S Flower Street/6th Street, T 213 892 8080, www.standardhotels.com*

SLS Hotel Beverly Hills
Sam Nazarian called on Philippe Starck
to reimagine the old Le Méridien as
the 297-room SLS. As you might expect,
there are lots of fun elements here,
including pool tables on each floor.
The rooms, such as the Premier King
(pictured), strike the right balance
between comfort and style.
465 S La Cienega Boulevard,
T 310 247 0400, www.slshotels.com

Avalon Beverly Hills

Kelly Wearstler's tribute to midcentury modern chic – all George Nelson lamps and Isamu Noguchi tables – opened in 1999. It soon became the hippest spot to hang out in Beverly Hills and still draws a big crowd of beautiful folk. Built from the bones of the old Beverly Carlton, once a haunt of Marilyn's, plus two adjoining apartment blocks, it was designed as an open-plan space, and some of the guest rooms open on to balconies overlooking the pool and its private, *cipollino*-marbled cabanas (above and opposite). Pea-green accents in a few of these and in the public spaces mute the slightly sub-*Jetsons* feel of the hotel furnishings. In 2010, Wearstler also revamped the lounge and restaurant, now called Oliverio (T 310 407 7791), which serves modern Italian food. The general vibe here manages to be fun but classy.
9400 W Olympic Boulevard, T 310 277 5221, www.avalonbeverlyhills.com

Chateau Marmont

This eccentric 1927 folly, perched above Sunset Boulevard, is one of our favourite LA hotels. The defining characteristic of André Balazs' restored château is not the fact that John Belushi's life ended here, but that it can boast private bungalows, a lovely pool and lush gardens, overlooked by arched colonnades (opposite). And if you grow weary of these delights, settle into the lounge on the first floor, where things are low-key and celeb-packed but convivial, compared with the frequently overrun Bar Marmont (T 323 650 0575). Of course, there are hotels with better rooms and bigger pools, and some place somewhere will be generating more buzz. But this is the Chateau Marmont – and there isn't anywhere else quite like it. *8221 Sunset Boulevard, T 323 656 1010, www.chateaumarmont.com*

Mr C
Murano chandeliers and a glass pool table by Nottage greet guests on arrival in Mr C's eclectic lobby, filled with hunter-green chesterfields and Eames recliners. The singular 12-storey hotel's 137 rooms (Mr C Suite, pictured) are inspired by European luxury yachts, down to the dark hardwood floors and rosewood cabinets. Each has a balcony.
1224 Beverwil Drive, T 310 277 2800

24 HOURS
SEE THE BEST OF THE CITY IN JUST ONE DAY

The 'drive everywhere' cliché about LA is so oft-repeated that it's easy to forget you will have to walk once you get to where you're going. Downtown, Beverly Hills, Santa Monica and Venice all have strollable streets, some of them pedestrianised, and the Venice Canals can only be appreciated on foot. There are shops you'll want to amble past, such as American Rag (150 S La Brea Avenue, T 323 935 3154), which has a great vintage section, and spots you'll visit on a whim, like R23 (923 E 2nd Street, T 213 687 7178) – a sushi joint with chairs by Frank Gehry. You can also walk the trails in Griffith Park or hike along the western end of Mulholland Drive.

All the same, to do LA in a day you must put in some serious tarmac time. We suggest starting in Venice (opposite), then heading up the Pacific Coast Highway to relax on the beach for a couple of hours. In a renewed frame of mind, make your way to Midtown for lunch at Tavern (see p055). Devote the afternoon to the arts by first visiting Regen Projects (6750 Santa Monica Boulevard, T 310 276 5424), a 930 sq m contemporary art space. Next, head to LACMA (see p036), followed by the Architecture and Design Museum (6032 Wilshire Boulevard, T 323 932 9393) across the street. End your day by going bowling at The Spare Room (see p038) and nursing a nightcap courtesy of the suave bartenders at Bar Stella (3932 W Sunset Boulevard, T 323 666 0265).

For full addresses, see Resources.

09.00 Intelligentsia Venice

Chicago-born coffee house Intelligentsia originally launched in LA in 2007 with a branch in Silver Lake. Two years later, a second outlet opened in Venice, in a space created by Ana Henton of MASS Architecture and Design. Awarded an American Institute of Architects award in 2010, the interior is more warehouse than coffee bar. With no traditional serving counter or tables, the coffee-making and drinking here is up close and personal. On entering, a barista will take you to an espresso machine and prepare your order in front of you, while you sit at one of the five bars asking as many questions as you wish. The coffee beans at Intelligentsia are scrupulously selected and there's a seasonal menu of teas on the menu too. *1331 Abbot Kinney Boulevard, T 310 399 1233, www.intelligentsiacoffee.com*

12.30 Matthew Marks Gallery

Artsy Angelenos were justifiably curious when influential New York gallery Matthew Marks opened in 2012 on a residential street in West Hollywood, far from the Culver City art crowds. This magnificently reductive 280 sq m space was designed by SoCal native Peter Zellner and his award-winning firm Zellnerplus. With a gentle nod to Ed Ruscha's photographic tome *Every Building on the Sunset Strip*, Zellner stuccoed the exterior of the windowless gallery, which is adorned with a 12m-long horizontal Ellsworth Kelly sculpture (*Black Bar for a Wall*, above). Skylights funnel light into two rooms, where you can find work by artists such as Gary Hume, Nan Goldin, Ken Price and the aforementioned Kelly (*Black Form*, opposite).
1062 N Orange Grove, T 323 654 1830, www.matthewmarks.com

14.30 LACMA

The ongoing transformation of LACMA started to take shape in 2008 with the launch of its Renzo Piano-designed Broad Contemporary Art Museum (BCAM), which provided LA with a major collection of contemporary and pop art. Exhibitions are drawn from the extensive collection of Eli and Edythe Broad, and include pieces by Warhol, Roy Lichtenstein, Cindy Sherman and Jeff Koons – all displayed among a maze of red-steel staircases or in the open-air pavilion. The LACMA complex, which sprawls over eight hectares, received a further boost in 2010 in the form of Piano's 4,180 sq m Resnick Pavilion (pictured), one of the largest purpose-built, naturally lit, open-plan museum spaces in the world. *5905 Wilshire Boulevard, T 323 857 6000, www.lacma.org*

20.00 The Spare Room

This chic gaming parlour, replete with a vintage 1940s two-lane bowling alley (above) and dozens of retro board games, is the brainchild of local after-hours legends Marc Rose and Med Abrous. Located in the Hollywood Roosevelt hotel, the intimate mezzanine-level space, which has views of the 75-year-old Grauman's Chinese Theatre (see p064), features an eye-catching art deco vanity-turned-DJ-booth, and custom-made backgammon tables. Those opting to bowl will have the chance to don the $800 bespoke George Esquivel shoes provided. Cocktails, like the bourbon-based Kentucky Glove Box, may affect scores, but it's worth the risk. The venue opens on Mondays 7pm to 2am, and Wednesday to Saturday 8pm to 2am. *7000 Hollywood Boulevard, T 323 769 7296, www.spareroomhollywood.com*

22.00 Umamicatessen

Adam Fleischman, founder of LA's Umami Burger (T 323 931 3000), introduced this multi-stationed restaurant to the city in 2012. Although the main focus is firmly on Umami's celebrated buns (try a Manly Burger with beer-infused cheddar), the space also contains four separate kitchens and a bar, including a kosher-style deli (The Cure), a fried-to-order doughnut stand (And a Donut) and a coffee shop (Spring for Coffee). Seating 170, the eaterie is based in an industrial dining hall at the Orpheum Theatre, where local design firm SO|DA lined sections of the walls with wood from a 1930s distillery in Alabama. Arrive early to stake your claim at the Back Bar and order our favourite cocktail, the Teal Goose (vodka, celery, kiwi and truffle salt). *852 S Broadway, T 213 413 8626, www.umami.com*

URBAN LIFE
CAFÉS, RESTAURANTS, BARS AND NIGHTCLUBS

If you're looking to suck up some glamour, few places can compete with LA's Cahuenga Boulevard, Hollywood Boulevard or Sunset Strip. With a few noble exceptions, LA's restaurant scene was never really about the cooking, although that changed thanks to eateries such as Mario Batali's Osteria Mozza (6602 Melrose Avenue, T 323 297 0100) and Todd English's Beso (6350 Hollywood Boulevard, T 323 467 7991). When it is just the food that matters, try Animal (435 N Fairfax Avenue, T 323 782 9225) for a carnivorous feast from chefs Jon Shook and Vinny Dotolo, or Italian eaterie Gjelina (1429 Abbot Kinney Boulevard, T 310 450 1429) in Venice. Nearby, the once sleepy district of Mar Vista is now home to chef-driven restaurants like the incredibly hip A-Frame (see p042), and in and around Culver City you'll find gems such as Sang Yoon's South-East Asian Lukshon (3239 Helms Avenue T 310 202 6808).

Further north in West Hollywood, where the vibe is more flashy, trendy bars and restaurants, like Laurel Hardware (7984 Santa Monica Boulevard, T 323 656 6070), are everywhere. And then there's the question of where to find the best burger joint: some say it's In-N-Out (7009 Sunset Boulevard, T 1 800 786 1000); others swear by Umamicatessen (see p039). Local treasures also include Pink's Hot Dogs (709 N La Brea Avenue, T 323 931 4223) or Roscoe's House of Chicken 'n' Waffles (1514 N Gower Street, T 323 466 7453). *For full addresses, see Resources.*

Tsujita

Perched on a corner in a neighbourhood nicknamed Little Osaka, chef Takehiro Tsujita's artisan noodle house is known for *tsukemen*: undressed noodles that diners dip in an intensely porky broth. With outposts in Tokyo and Bangkok, the 2011 opening of this branch of Tsujita was eagerly awaited by Angelenos. Designed by architect Takeshi Sano of Tokyo-based firm SWeeT, the interiors are inspired by the landscape surrounding the Izumo shrine in Japan, and the ceiling comprises 2,500 wooden sticks cut in varying lengths to mimic the sensation of rolling clouds. Glowing paper lanterns cast a warm light. Signature ramen and *tsukemen* are only available during lunch; dinner focuses on *izakaya* specialties and a rare sake list. *2057 Sawtelle Boulevard, T 310 231 7373, www.tsujita-la.com*

A-Frame
Few places can speak of the booming LA food culture like A-Frame. Designed by Sean Knibb, the space is a mix of Jean Prouvé chairs, custom picnic tables and concrete banquettes. The 'godfather' of the LA food truck movement, Roy Choi, is in charge, sending out dishes such as octopus with carrot *gochujang* purée.
12565 W Washington Boulevard,
T 310 398 7700, www.aframela.com

Comme Ça

Inspired by the brasseries of France, chef David Myers, who earned a Michelin star at Sona, has scored another hit with the elegant Comme Ça. The crisp interiors by LA's KAA Design Group include long blackboards set against white buttoned banquettes, antique mirrors and a picture ledge filled with culinary artwork. The menu is rooted in Gallic classics, such as steak-frites and onion soup. There is also an extensive cocktail list; we like La Dame Épicée, concocted with Arette Reposado tequila, blackberries and serrano chillies. Comme Ça's no-reservation raw bar is an excellent place to call in for some oysters and a glass of fizz, or alternatively you could order from the cheese counter and grab a table in the back room.
8479 Melrose Avenue, T 323 782 1104, www.commecarestaurant.com

Red O

Touted as America's finest exponent of Mexican cuisine, famed Chicago chef Rick Bayless (Frontera Grill, Topolobampo, Xoco) oversees this buzzy venue that opened in 2010. Critics were always going to be tough on a new Mexican eaterie in town, but Red O has proved to be a success, thanks to Bayless' exemplary regional cooking. A collaboration between G+ Gulla Jonsdottir Design and Dodd Mitchell, it is enclosed in a steel cage, making for a dramatic entrance to the lofty interior, with its soaring ceiling, glass tequila tunnel and bar carved out of rock. For drinks, be brave and take a seat at one of the bar swings, or kick back on the daybed. The preppy staff come dressed in custom-made shirts, Levi's and Adidas trainers. *8155 Melrose Avenue, T 323 655 5009, www.redorestaurant.com*

Superba Snack Bar

Proprietor Paul Hibler joined forces with chef Jason Neroni in 2012 to open this 'postmodern pasteria'. Located on Rose Avenue, which locals are calling the new Abbot Kinney, Superba is a no-reservation, bohemian neighbourhood joint, serving house-made pastas and small plates. LA-based experimental architectural firm Design, Bitches took its cues from the artsy community, creating an airy, playful interior that includes tiled banquettes upholstered with ponchos bought from the Venice boardwalk, and wallpaper by local artist Geoff McFetridge that depicts intermingling hands. The best seat in the house is at the bar, where you can spy Neroni playing with his pasta maker, or, as he calls it, 'the adult Play-Doh machine'. *533 Rose Avenue, T 310 399 6400, www.superbasnackbar.com*

The Parlour Room

Racing-green wallpaper, antique gold mirrors and deep, tufted sofas give this Hollywood bar a fabulously dark and decadent feel. Opened by Craig Trager of the Vintage Bar Group, which owns five other hotspots, including No Bar (T 818 753 0545) and The Woods (T 323 876 6612), The Parlour Room is just off the Cahuenga corridor. The area is home to a cluster of clubby lounges and watering holes; SBE's The Colony (T 323 525 2450) is round the corner. Sit at the front bar (above) or snag one of the sofas and indulge in some prime people-watching in the flattering glow of the chandeliers. There's another bar at the back, displaying a collection of vintage bourbon decanters. Open every night until 2am.

6423 Yucca Street, T 323 463 0609, www.vintagebargroup.com

Lamill Coffee

The coolest coffee shop on the east side, Lamill was designed by Rubbish Interiors, which fitted the space with a glamorous mix of gilded chandeliers and buttoned faux-leather chairs, winning a 2008 American Institute of Architects award in the process. The beverages are similarly elaborate – try a cup of siphon-brewed joe or a coffee infused with a brioche flavour. But Lamill is more than a coffee shop – also on offer are stronger brews like the Black & Black (half-stout, half-iced coffee), Bloody Mary made with *soju*, and tea champagne. The food menu was devised by two-Michelin-starred Michael Cimarusti of Providence (T 323 460 4170). For a power breakfast, look for the warm brioche doughnuts with vanilla cream.
1636 Silver Lake Boulevard,
T 323 663 4441, www.lamillcoffee.com

Playa

Chef John Rivera Sedlar has sated locals since 2011 with a sizeable menu of pan-Latin small plates, helpfully divided into 'cool' and 'warm' to simplify things. Architect Osvaldo Maiozzi dotted Playa's ceilings with skylights, while straw chandeliers, which are shaped like sea urchins, also add a startling touch. *7360 Beverly Boulevard, T 323 933 5300, www.playarivera.com*

The Eveleigh

Australian-born chef Jordan Toft delivers European and American gastro-pub fare in this 1920s former private house. The rustic setting is amplified by touches such as an old cobblers' chest, vintage leather chairs and flooring made from the salvaged wood of a 19th-century church. Half the eaterie is perched on an open-air terrace filled with lime and olive trees, and surrounded by sprawling city views.

A Milk & Honey disciple, the head barman David Kupchinsky's inventive cocktails include Poor Carlito, a mix of tequila, lime, honey and sea salt. Those looking for simple libations not listed on the menu will be met with a gruff 'no'. However, the drinks that are served here are delicious enough to permit the attitude.
8752 Sunset Boulevard, T 424 239 1630, www.theeveleigh.com

Black Hogg

In 2012, chef-owner Eric Park opened this venue in a former Chinese restaurant in Silver Lake. In charge of the overhaul was industrial designer Brendan Ravenhill, who cited Alvar Aalto's Finnish pavilion at the 1939 New York World's Fair as a reference point for the interiors and furnishings. Vertical white oak plywood strips line the stark yet surprisingly intimate dining room, and custom-designed LEDs, constructed from wood and paper, illuminate grey walls and concrete floors. The clapboard bar (above), adorned with mirrors found in fleamarkets, is often packed with locals, who are usually found devouring Park's pork belly tacos with Fuji apple slaw and jalapeno relish, and the popular deep-fried 'popcorn bacon'. Closed on Sundays. *2852 W Sunset Boulevard, T 323 953 2820, www.blackhogg.com*

Hatfield's

Husband-and-wife chefs Quinn and Karen Hatfield reopened their Michelin-starred restaurant at its new address in 2010, doubling its size in the process. Just like the space, created by local designer Alexis Readinger of Preen, their contemporary American cooking also seems a little bolder and keeps LA's foodies coming back for more; we recommend the date- and mint-crusted lamb with potato chive purée, or a croque madame with prosciutto and yellowtail. Readinger chose wide-plank flooring and a palette of acorn, flint, olive and walnut for the interior, lighting the main dining area (above) with a linen chandelier modelled on the chemical components of honey. The large bar serves fabulous cocktails. *6703 Melrose Avenue, T 323 935 2977, www.hatfieldsrestaurant.com*

Tavern

Chef Suzanne Goin and sommelier Caroline Styne form one of LA's most dynamic and successful culinary duos, and their Californian-Mediterranean café/restaurant Tavern in Brentwood has been packed since it opened in 2009. Pick up a picnic box from The Larder, a deli section at the front, or eat in the light-filled dining room (above). Santa Monica-based Jeffrey Alan Marks topped the counters in the deli with white Silestone, whereas a grey stone dominates the bar area. California oak flooring runs throughout. Marks designed the furniture too; the chairs are upholstered with blue sun-bleached denim by Rose Tarlow. Goin and Styne also run AOC (T 323 653 6359) and Lucques (T 323 655 6277) in West Hollywood. *11648 San Vicente Boulevard, T 310 806 6464, www.tavernla.com*

Ray's

This glass and concrete eaterie is the final piece in Renzo Piano's LACMA trilogy (see p036). Mediterranean cuisine is served among furniture by Eero Saarinen and Charles and Ray Eames. Ranged on the walls are teacups from the museum's Ellen Palevsky Cup Collection, which spans 1850 to 1950.
LACMA, 5905 Wilshire Boulevard, T 323 857 6180, www.patinagroup.com

Soho House

Brainchild of Nick Jones, who also brought Cecconi's to LA, this London import has taken over the top floors of Luckman Plaza on the Strip. The country-chic interiors are the work of Waldo Fernandez together with Jones, while Matthew Armistead, formerly of London's River Café, is chef. As you climb the sweeping marble staircase up to the bar and sitting room, it is clear that this private members' club is aimed at refined socialising rather than rowdy parties. The lounge is as busy for breakfast as it is for dinner at 9pm, and is the ideal retreat for afternoon tea among the books and vintage furnishings. The terrace garden (above), planted with California olive trees, boasts superb views and provides a discreet spot for business or pleasure. *9200 Sunset Boulevard, T 310 432 9200, www.sohohousewh.com*

WP24

In the centre of the LA Live entertainment district, Wolfgang Puck's 2010 restaurant at the top of The Ritz-Carlton can't be beaten for its stellar views. The 24th-floor space was designed by LA firm ICRAVE to appeal to a younger crowd, without alienating the hotel's loyal clientele. Grey and purple hues soften the effect of the metal pendants. There are two dining rooms, a wine room and a lounge, which is a superb place for an aperitif. Puck is lauded for his modern Chinese cuisine and WP24 has received top-flight reviews since its opening. Try the signature dish, stir-fried Kobe beef. For Puck's take on modern Cali cuisine, book a table at Wolfgang Puck at Hotel Bel-Air (see p017), on the other side of town.
900 W Olympic Boulevard, T 213 743 8824, www.wolfgangpuck.com

The Penthouse

Once part of a dowdy chain, The Huntley is now one of the plushest hotels on the west side. Exotic design flourishes include a lobby with wooden drum tables, African fertility chairs and a check-in counter topped with inlaid stingray skin. But the real draw here has to be The Penthouse restaurant and lounge, which has an ethereal ambience thanks to its white decor and views stretching from Malibu to Palos Verdes. One of the best places in LA to watch the sun go down, this is where the Santa Monica elite start their evening, at the oval bar, mojito in hand. Hit up the restaurant at the weekend to sample its brunch menu, which features elegantly turned-out, hangover-friendly dishes like huevos rancheros and corned beef hash. *The Huntley Hotel, 1111 2nd Street, T 310 393 8080, www.thehuntleyhotel.com*

INSIDER'S GUIDE

JAY EZRA NAYSSAN, REAL ESTATE ENTREPRENEUR

Jay Ezra Nayssan is that rarest of beasts: a native Angeleno. Based in Little Osaka, he likes to divide his time between architectural photography and managing Nayssan Properties, an all-inclusive real-estate firm combining interior design and architecture. For inspiration, he looks to Pierre Koenig's Stahl House (1635 Woods Drive, T 323 744 1635) in the Hollywood Hills: 'Its cantilevered foundation, seamless glass walls and elegant simplicity remind me that LA is, and always has been, a city of the future,' he says. On the first Sunday of each month, Nayssan treks east to hunt for bargains at the outdoor Pasadena City College Flea Market (1570 E Colorado Boulevard, T 626 585 7906). He also likes to shop at boutiques such as Weltenbuerger (1764 N Vermont Avenue, T 323 300 5990), for cutting-edge fashion labels like Ermie.

When eating out, he loves the *omakase*-only Sushi Park (8539 W Sunset Boulevard, T 310 652 0523) but, for more basic bites, he packs a picnic and heads to the Hollywood Forever Cemetery (6000 Santa Monica Boulevard, T 323 469 1181), where Cinespia projects classic films. For a more strenuous outdoor activity, Nayssan climbs the steps at Malibu's hidden El Matador State Beach (32215 Pacific Coast Highway): 'Head in the direction of the Pacific, and you'll find yourself on top of a magnificent cliff, looking down on to incredible rocks jetting out of the ocean,' he says.

For full addresses, see Resources.

ARCHITOUR
A GUIDE TO LA'S ICONIC BUILDINGS

As befits the city of the second chance, the built environment of Los Angeles has been constantly reinvented and reformulated, with a dizzying disregard for the past. Only a few poor adobe buildings date from the city's foundation; and then there's the Bradbury Building (304 S Broadway, T 213 626 1893), one of the few 19th-century structures still standing. After WWI, Los Angeles began to expand and established its indiscriminately exotic (okay, chaotic) look. Everything from reinterpreted haciendas to Beaux Arts Egyptian tombs were put up. This was the period of Grauman's Chinese Theatre (6801 Hollywood Boulevard, T 323 461 3331) and the pyramid-topped City Hall (200 N Spring Street).

No architour could do the city justice without taking in the midcentury domestic buildings designed by Frank Lloyd Wright and his disciples, Richard Neutra, Rudolph Schindler and John Lautner. Highlights include Wright's Hollyhock House (see p070) and Ennis House (2655 Glendower Avenue), used as a set for *Blade Runner*, Neutra's Lovell Health House (4616 Dundee Drive) and Schindler's former home (see p066) in West Hollywood. In 1949, Lautner's wood-and-glass design for a coffee shop called Googie's on Sunset Strip spawned a new, futuristic style of architecture. A lot of Googie gems still exist in Los Angeles, one of the most characterful being Norms Restaurant (see p012).

For full addresses, see Resources.

Samitaur Tower

Once a dull industrial 'burb, Culver City is fast morphing into a media and business hotspot, thanks in part to developers Frederick and Laurie Samitaur Smith. The husband and wife team have been on a mission to regenerate the area, commissioning adventurous buildings such as this 'art pavilion'. Completed in 2010, it was designed by architects Eric Owen Moss, who have collaborated with the Samitaur Smiths on other projects in the area. Set on one of the city's main arteries, the eye-catching structure comprises a series of stacked offset volumes, separated by steel rings, and each storey features a screen displaying art and graphics. At 22m high, it's an instant beacon, with observation decks offering great views over LA.

Hayden Avenue/National Boulevard

Schindler House

Modernist architect Rudolph Schindler
redefined the contemporary California
home with this avant-garde residence
and studio, completed in 1922. It's a
single-storey structure, with an open
floor-plan, large sliding doors, clerestory
windows and tranquil patios. Today,
the MAK Center for Art and Architecture
hosts exhibitions and concerts here.
835 N Kings Road, T 323 651 1510

Chemosphere

Julius Shulman's iconic photographs might have made this John Lautner building a bit too familiar for some, but there's no substitute for seeing first hand what an architect of genius could do with a tiny budget of £17,000, in a vertiginous, mountainside location. The 45-degree slope imposed constraints, but apparently none at all to Lautner's imagination. For years, it had a 'For Sale' sign up and was parodied on *The Simpsons* as the mad, modern monstrosity that no one would buy, although it was eventually sold. Architect Frank Escher was hired by the new owner to restore the Chemosphere to something approaching its original state, a revamp that earned the property a prestigious award from the Los Angeles Conservancy. Today, Lautner's classic stands as a symbol of 1960s optimism and of today's midcentury real-estate mania.
776 Torreyson Drive

Hollyhock House

Sitting on top of a hill in Barnsdall Park, Hollyhock House was Frank Lloyd Wright's first LA-based project, taking advantage of what he coined 'California Romanza': the freedom to make one's own form. Built between 1919 and 1921, Wright's design created a stunning house and garden while developing a regional style of SoCal architecture. Making full use of the local climate, the living space extends outdoors with a courtyard and terraces. Named after the favourite flower of its former owner, oil heiress Aline Barnsdall, the house is dotted with hollyhock motifs. In 1927, in memory of her father, Theodore Barnsdall, Aline donated the house and 11 acres of land to the city of Los Angeles for use as a public arts complex.
4800 Hollywood Boulevard,
T 323 644 6269, www.hollyhockhouse.net

SHOPPING

THE BEST RETAIL THERAPY AND WHAT TO BUY

As with most things in LA, the problem with shopping here is the excess of choice. The highest density of clothing and homewares shops lies in West Hollywood, running from Robertson Boulevard in the west to La Brea Avenue in the east, and along Beverly Boulevard, Melrose Avenue and Melrose Place. This is where you'll find the Hollywood Regency Phyllis Morris showroom (655 N Robertson Boulevard, T 310 289 6868), as well as Blackman Cruz (836 N Highland Avenue, T 323 466 8600). Don't overlook Iko Iko (931 N Fairfax Avenue, T 323 719 1079) and, if you're in the trade, some showrooms in Cesar Pelli's Pacific Design Center (8687 Melrose Avenue, T 310 657 0800) may sell to you.

On the fashion scene, check out the leather bags at RTH (537 N La Cienega Boulevard, T 310 289 7911), then continue down to boutique-filled Beverly Boulevard, stopping in at Garde (No 7418, T 323 424 4667) for accessories and home furnishings. The Los Feliz/Silver Lake border is packed with quirky shops, including Soap Plant/Wacko/La Luz de Jesus (4633 Hollywood Boulevard, T 323 663 0122), which sells kitsch collectables. In Venice, you could lose half a day on Abbot Kinney Boulevard alone. Visit Surfing Cowboys (No 1624, T 310 450 4891) for vintage furniture and ephemera, browse the homewares at Tortoise (see p080), or take in the exhibitions at nearby L&M Arts (see p082).

For full addresses, see Resources.

Poketo

After almost a decade online, Poketo has finally opened a bricks-and-mortar store in the funky Downtown Arts District – and it's hard to miss the oversized, hanging cardboard letters spelling out Poketo in the store window, announcing its arrival. Husband-and-wife team Ted Vadakan and Angie Myung founded the brand in San Francisco in 2003. Since then, it's become known for its accessible, affordable items, including a line of collectable vinyl wallets designed in collaboration with a variety of illustrators such as Portland's Kate Bingaman Burt and SoCal's Tim Biskup. Design-driven wares, such as brass bottle-openers by Oji Masanori and Japanese washi tape, are artfully displayed on tables constructed from MDF doors.
820 E 3rd Street, T 213 537 0751, www.poketo.com

ARCANA: Books on the Arts

In 2012, Lee and Whitney Kaplan moved their iconic bookstore from Santa Monica, where it had operated since the 1980s, to Culver City's former Helms Bakery, which now houses design outlets such as Vitra (T 310 839 3400). With myriad thriving galleries nearby, this was the perfect location for a shop specialising in rare art catalogues and tomes on architecture, photography and interior design. Mark Lee, of architects Johnston Marklee, designed the 408 sq m monochromatic space. It is split into three volumes, with punctured black walls and glossy white concrete floors. Shelving by Brock Mayeux, of design firm Landlocd, expands to create a huge black body of books, reminiscent of a shifting Tony Smith sculpture.
8675 Washington Boulevard,
T 310 458 1499, www.arcanabooks.com

Malibu Lumber Yard

This 2,800 sq m shopping mall, opened in 2009, is one of LA's green success stories. Renovated by developer Richard Weintraub and landscaper Richard Sperber, the complex incorporates reclaimed materials from the lumber yard that once stood here. Waste water is recycled to irrigate a neighbouring park, while vertical and roof gardens help reduce heat absorption. Shop at tony stores such as Maxfield, which also has a branch on Melrose Avenue (see p085), Tory Burch and James Perse, and grab a bite at eco-friendly eaterie Café Habana (T 310 317 0300). Or take a power break in the decked courtyard (above), with its salt-water fish tanks and living-room-style seating, and watch the celebs go by. *3939 Cross Creek Road, www.themalibulumberyard.com*

Church Boutique

Owners Rodney Burns and David Malvaney hand-pick a range of multitalented, ahead-of-the-curve designers for this unique lifestyle boutique, featuring everything from fashion and jewellery to furniture. Occupying a 465 sq m loft, discreetly hidden behind a veil of vines, the store carries more than 50 lines that cater to both men and women, including the LA-based Balatsos, which specialises in metal-spiked shoulder bags and clutches, and the Canadian label Mandula, which makes one-of-a-kind womenswear pieces. As thought-provoking as the clothes on sale here are the store layout – which often features dresses hanging from the ceiling or sitting on top of vintage furniture – and the walls filled with contemporary art. *7277 Santa Monica Boulevard, T 323 876 8887, www.churchboutique.com*

Our Favorite Shop
Named after The Style Council's 1985
album, this is the first outlet for Sung
Choi's stylish men's footwear company,
CLAE. Shelving dissected into movable
forms is populated with the brand's
latest styles, alongside other labels such
as Claw Money and Baron Von Fancy,
design books and grooming products.
5455 W Pico Boulevard, T 323 930 0347,
www.ourfavoriteshop.com

Tortoise

Covetable Japanese wares are the draw at Tortoise, owned by Keiko and Taku Shinomoto. The couple moved to LA in 2003 and wanted to gather together products designed to last (the tortoise is a symbol of longevity in Japan). They have chosen both functional and decorative items, including handmade tea canisters from Kyoto, driftwood birds from Tokyo, and ceramics from all over the country.

The store also sells vintage vases, plates and fabrics, as well as out-of-print art and photography books. It also hosts the odd exhibition. Some items are only available in the Shinomotos' first shop, Tortoise General Store (T 310 314 8448), including this plywood clock (above), $85, by Mori Toyoshi for Lemnos. *1342 Abbot Kinney Boulevard, T 310 396 7335, www.tortoiselife.com*

L&M Arts
The second branch of the blue-chip L&M gallery, featuring artists such as Thomas Houseago (pictured) and Paul McCarthy, opened in 2010 in a former 1930s Venice Beach power plant adjoined to a new structure by wHY Architecture's Kulapat Yantrasast. The garden that connects the two doubles as an exhibition space. *660 S Venice Boulevard, T 310 821 6400, www.lmgallery.com*

Heath Ceramics

Founded by Edith Heath in Sausalito in 1948, Heath Ceramics pushed the ideas of good design and responsible, waste-averse production long before they became fashionable. In 2003, industrial designer Catherine Bailey and her husband, Robin Petravic, a mechanical engineer, bought the company from the ailing Heath. In 2008, intent on re-energising the brand, they opened in LA, inviting potter Adam Silverman to be the studio director. His connections among the city's artistic elite helped push the profile of ceramic art in Los Angeles. Housed in an art deco building, the airy interiors, by local firm Commune Design, feature knotty pine millwork and fixtures – the perfect foil to Heath's colourful wares.

7525 Beverly Boulevard, T 323 965 0800, www.heathceramics.com

Maxfield

Don't be intimidated by the severe security guard at the entrance – this big, polished concrete building watched over by Roger Herman's *Ape* sculptures houses a smart concept store carrying a well-edited range of high-end fashion, accessories, jewellery and homewares. The window displays are no less eye-catching than the merchandise, which includes Rick Owens, Comme des Garçons and both new and vintage Chanel in the womenswear sections, as well as Balmain's hard-to-find menswear range. Discreet service and Beverly Hills price tags make this shop a favourite with celebs, so try not to stare if you bump into an Olsen twin. There's a second branch, Maxfield Gallery (T 310 275 8818), across the road, that specialises in furniture. *8825 Melrose Avenue, T 310 274 8800, www.maxfieldla.com*

Fred Segal

This LA stalwart is still a great one-stop shop in which to find hip local designers and accessories. Pick up a pair of Ron Herman jeans or pop into the Apothia section and choose from scents made from recherché ingredients such as Bulgarian rose and Javan vetiver. There are two other branches in Santa Monica. *8100 Melrose Avenue, T 323 655 3734, www.fredsegal.com*

SPORTS AND SPAS

WORK OUT, CHILL OUT OR JUST WATCH

Woody Allen was making jokes about LA's fitness fanaticism in the 1970s, and it hasn't got any less devout. Choices are dizzying and subject to rapidly changing trends. See and be seen at gyms such as Equinox (8590 W Sunset Boulevard, T 310 289 1900), or get your car washed while you exercise at 24 Hour Fitness (15301 Ventura Boulevard, T 818 728 6777). Exhale (Fairmont Miramar Hotel, 101 Wilshire Boulevard, T 310 319 3193) is the spot for a post-workout massage overlooking the sea. For a facial, book in at The Ritz-Carlton Spa (900 W Olympic Boulevard, T 213 743 8800), or, if you're a fan of high-tech treatments, make for Sonya Dakar Skin Clinic (9975 Santa Monica Boulevard, T 310 553 7344). Anastasia is the place to have your brows shaped – try the Brentwood branch (11933 Wilshire Boulevard, T 310 479 8300) – whereas the serene Mars the Salon (opposite) offers cutting-edge nail art, Tokyo style. Ciel Spa (see p090) is ideal for pre-party pampering.

Los Angeles has no NFL team, so baseball and basketball are the sporting passions here. The LA Lakers are the basketball team every other fan loves to hate and tickets to see them at Staples Center (1111 S Figueroa Street, T 213 742 7100) aren't cheap. Nearby LA Live (800 W Olympic Boulevard, T 866 548 3452) hosts some events too. As for baseball, the LA Dodgers have played at Dodger Stadium (1000 Elysian Park Avenue, T 323 224 1507) since 1962. *For full addresses, see Resources.*

Mars the Salon

Following the success of his Tokyo parlour, Mars the Salon owner Hiroko Fujikawa brought the Japanese craftsmanship of nail care to West Hollywood. The unisex venue, in LA's design district, attracts a fashion-forward crowd seeking unique luxury manicures administered by highly trained Japanese technicians. Private rooms, which have a grey-and-white colour palette, feel fresh and sedate, and clients are treated with organic towels, built-in porcelain foot baths, and HD TVs with headphones, should they wish to tune out. We suggest you recline in one of the custom-made leather chairs and give your manicurist free range to craft animal prints, barcodes or a seasonal motif on to your talons. Closed Sundays and Mondays. *606 Westmount Drive, T 310 652 0930, www.mars-salon.com*

Ciel Spa at SLS

There's a dreamy quality to the Philippe Starck-designed spa at the SLS Hotel (see p024). Perhaps it's the all-white interior and the sheer drapery or the giant floating ottoman in the changing room – all designed to transport you far away from the smog beyond. The six suites include one for couples, which has side-by-side soaking tubs, while the techie Acoustic Sound Resonance Therapy beds with iPod docks aim to make you feel as though music is flowing through your body. The massages are excellent and there are edible boosts on offer too: try the weekend Brunch & Massage package or the healthy snacks from chef José Andrés' restaurant, Bazaar, downstairs. Or have your spa valet make you a soothing infusion by Dr Tea.
465 S La Cienega Boulevard,
T 310 246 5560, www.cielatsls.com

Annenberg Community Beach House

On the edge of Santa Monica Bay, this $27.5m, LEED gold-certified project has won several accolades, including a Los Angeles Conservancy Preservation Award. A design team, which included luminaries such as Frederick Fisher and Partners, Mia Lehrer + Associates, Roy McMakin, AdamsMorioka, Charles Pankow Builders and the Historic Resources Group, transformed the site, which includes a museum, an event space, a pool (pictured) and a restaurant. A hotspot in the 1920s, the estate was built by William Randolph Hearst for the actress Marion Davies who, in turn, hosted guests like Charlie Chaplin and Greta Garbo. The pool is only open on summer weekends, from 10am to 4pm. *415 Pacific Coast Highway, T 310 458 4904, www.annenbergbeachhouse.com*

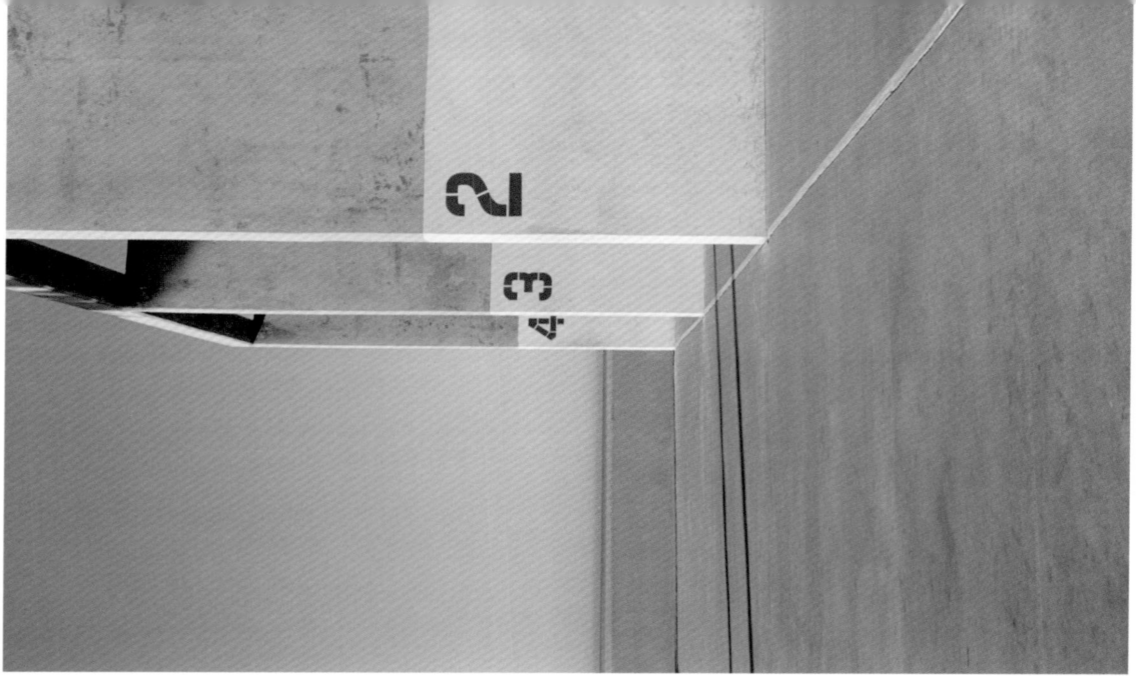
2
3
4

Venice Beach Recreation Center
Despite the tie-dyed tat and tattoo-tastic feeling to the Venice boardwalk, it would be a shame for any fit folk to come to LA and not visit the ocean-front sports area, better known as Muscle Beach. Set up in 1934 in neighbouring Santa Monica as a government-funded training ground for gymnasts, stunt people, wrestlers, acrobats, weightlifters and circus performers, Muscle Beach claims to be where all modern gyms have their origin. The site moved to Venice in the 1960s, but continued to attract the bodies beautiful and those who just wanted to watch. Today, as well as the pumped-up displays of physical prowess, the recreation zone offers basketball, tennis, handball and volleyball courts – if you feel like joining in, you can book through the Center. *1800 Ocean Front Walk, T 310 399 2775, www.laparks.org*

ESCAPES

WHERE TO GO IF YOU WANT TO LEAVE TOWN

This being a mega-city, it's tempting to think there's enough to see in LA County without going any further, but the surrounding area has plenty to tempt you on to the freeways or commuter planes out of town. The most scenic route north is the Pacific Coast Highway, which will take you to Spanish-flavoured Santa Barbara. If you have time, take a diversion to the idyllic town of Ojai (pronounced 'Oh-hi') at the foot of the Topa Topa Mountains.

Heading south, you get to pleasant San Diego, with its buzzy downtown – stay at Hotel Palomar (1047 5th Avenue, T 619 515 3000), or the Andaz (600 F Street, T 619 849 1234) in the historic Gaslamp Quarter. If you're driving, there are a number of towns worth exploring along the way, including La Jolla (pronounced 'La Hoya'), home of Louis Khan's Salk Institute (see p100).

Palm Springs is a popular getaway, known for its midcentury modern architecture, fabled private villas (see p098) and hip hotels – try the Ace (701 E Palm Canyon Drive, T 760 325 9900) or The Horizon (1050 E Palm Canyon Drive, T 760 323 1858). Then there's Mexico. It's a 40-minute drive from San Diego Airport to the wine region of Baja California and hotels such as Grupo Habita's 20-cabin Endémico (Carretera Tecate-Ensenada, km75, T +52 646 155 2775). If you have more time, head deeper into the country, to the Mayan Riviera (see p102) on the Yucatán Peninsula. *For full addresses, see Resources.*

PMCA, Pasadena

For an easy day trip, the pretty city of Pasadena in the San Gabriel Valley is a short 16km drive from Downtown. Make a beeline for the Pasadena Museum of California Art (PMCA). Opened in 2002, the gallery was designed by LA-based architects Johnson Favaro to provide a cultural centrepiece for the regeneration of the downtown neighbourhood and historic Playhouse District. An open-air staircase leads up to the lobby (above), gallery spaces, the bookshop and a roof terrace, which has great views of the San Gabriel Mountains. Exhibitions are dedicated solely to Californian art, design and architecture from 1850 to the present (*Petal Ceiling Treatment* by Studio Lilica, above). Closed Mondays and Tuesdays. *490 E Union Street, T 626 568 3665, www.pmcaonline.org*

Twin Palms, Palm Springs

In 1947, Frank Sinatra commissioned the very first residential project by E Stewart Williams, a Californian architect who would help shape the image of Palm Springs as a bastion of modernist architecture. Few houses can compete with the mythical heights attained by Twin Palms, where the star lived with his second wife, Ava Gardner. A crack in the sink in the master bedroom has been left to preserve the moment when Sinatra supposedly threw a bottle of champagne at Gardner. When Eric Ellenbogen bought the place in 2005, he wanted to evoke the Sinatra era while giving the house a life of its own, which interior decorator Darren Brown achieved with an idiosyncratic mix of vintage furnishings and artwork. The house can now be rented through Beau Monde Villas. *T 877 318 2090, www.sinatrahouse.com*

Salk Institute, La Jolla

When the inventor of the first effective polio vaccine, Dr Jonas Salk, asked the Estonian-born architect Louis Kahn to design a research institute, he asked for somewhere that would be fit for Picasso. Perfection is rare in buildings, but Kahn's 1960s cast-concrete campus, set on the bluffs of La Jolla, is widely acknowledged to merit the accolade. Overlooking the Pacific, the complex is centred on a grand, open courtyard (pictured) made of travertine marble. It is flanked by two mirror-image structures, containing light-filled laboratories and professors' offices, many with unobstructed ocean views. Free tours are held on weekdays; call or register online two days in advance. *10010 N Torrey Pines Road, T 858 453 4100, www.salk.edu*

Be Tulum, Mexico

Designed by sibling architects Sebastian and Jere Sas, this beachside resort, close to the Mayan ruins of Tulum, is one of a clutch of properties to have opened on the Caribbean coast of Mexico in recent years. Located 120km south of Cancún Airport, near Playa del Carmen, Be Tulum has 20 spacious suites featuring local limestone, Bisazza mosaic tiles and warm touches such as Brazilian wood. Those on the ground floor have pools and a terrace, while the suites on upper levels feature balconies with jacuzzis. The Ocean Suites boast pools overlooking the UNESCO World Heritage Site of Sian Ka'an, a biosphere reserve. There is also a spa and a beach club/lounge bar (above) with an adjoining pool. Service is laidback, but spot-on.
Carretera Tulum, Quintana Roo,
T +52 187 7265 4139, www.betulum.com

NOTES

SKETCHES AND MEMOS

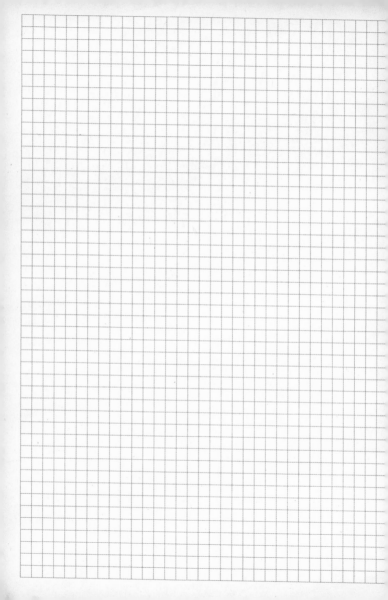

RESOURCES

CITY GUIDE DIRECTORY

The Woods 048
  1533 N La Brea Avenue
  T 323 876 6612
  www.vintagebargroup.com
WP24 059
  24th floor
  The Ritz-Carlton
  900 W Olympic Boulevard
  T 213 743 8824
  www.wolfgangpuck.com

HOTELS
ADDRESSES AND ROOM RATES

Ace Hotel 016
  Room rates:
  prices on request
  929 S Broadway
  www.acehotel.com

Ace Hotel 096
  Room rates:
  double, from $140
  701 E Palm Canyon Drive
  Palm Springs
  T 760 325 9900
  www.acehotel.com

Andaz San Diego 088
  Room rates:
  double, $160
  600 F Street
  San Diego
  T 619 849 1234
  www.sandiego.andaz.hyatt.com

Andaz West Hollywood 021
  Room rates:
  double, $305;
  Sunset View King Room, $315
  8401 Sunset Boulevard
  T 323 656 1234
  www.westhollywood.andaz.hyatt.com

Avalon Beverly Hills 026
  Room rates:
  double, from $325
  9400 W Olympic Boulevard
  T 310 277 5221
  www.avalonbeverlyhills.com

Be Tulum 102
  Room rates:
  suite, from $390;
  Ocean Suite, from $655
  Carretera Tulum
  Quintana Roo
  Mexico
  T +52 187 7265 4139
  www.betulum.com

Hotel Bel-Air 017
  Room rates:
  double, from $515;
  Presidential Suite, $15,000
  701 Stone Canyon Road
  T 310 472 1211
  www.hotelbelair.com

Chateau Marmont 028
  Room rates:
  suite, from $680;
  bungalow, from $2,540
  8221 Sunset Boulevard
  T 323 656 1010
  www.chateaumarmont.com

Endémico 096
  Room rates:
  double, from $185
  Carretera Tecate-Ensenada km75
  Valle de Guadalupe
  Ensenada
  Baja California
  Mexico
  T +52 646 155 2775
  www.designhotels.com/endemico

The Horizon Hotel 096
Room rates:
double, from $180
1050 E Palm Canyon Drive
Palm Springs
T 760 323 1858
www.thehorizonhotel.com

Mr C 030
Room rates:
double, from $390;
Mr C Suite, $1,300
1224 Beverwil Drive
T 310 277 2800
www.mrchotels.com

Palihotel 016
Room rates:
double, from $290
7950 Melrose Avenue
T 323 272 4588
www.pali-hotel.com

Palihouse 016
Room rates:
suite, from $420
8465 Holloway Drive
T 323 656 4100
www.palihouse.com

Hotel Palomar 096
Room rates:
double, from $185
1047 5th Avenue
San Diego
T 619 515 3000
www.hotelpalomar-sandiego.com

**The Redbury @ Hollywood
and Vine** 016
Room rates:
double, from $290
1717 Vine Street
T 323 962 1717
www.theredbury.com

Hotel Shangri-La 020
Room rates:
double, from $325;
suite, from $575;
Rock 'n' Roll Suite, from $575
1301 Ocean Avenue
T 310 394 2791
www.shangrila-hotel.com

SLS Hotel Beverly Hills 024
Room rates:
double, from $425;
Premier King Room, $705
465 S La Cienega Boulevard
T 310 247 0400
www.slshotels.com

The Standard Downtown 022
Room rates:
double, from $220;
Huge Room, from $345
550 S Flower Street/6th Street
T 213 892 8080
www.standardhotels.com

The Standard Hollywood 016
Room rates:
double, from $230
8300 Sunset Boulevard
T 323 650 9090
www.standardhotels.com

Twin Palms 098
Villa, $2,900
(three-night miminum stay)
Palm Springs
T 877 318 2090
www.sinatrahouse.com

WALLPAPER* CITY GUIDES

Executive Editor
Rachael Moloney

Editor
Ella Marshall
Authors
David John Dick
Carole Dixon
Marisa Mazria Katz

Art Director
Loran Stosskopf
Art Editor
Eriko Shimazaki
Designer
Mayumi Hashimoto
Map Illustrator
Russell Bell

Photography Editor
Elisa Merlo
Assistant Photography Editor
Nabil Butt

Chief Sub-Editor
Nick Mee
Sub-Editors
Julia Chadwick
Kevin Grant

Editorial Assistant
Emma Harrison

Interns
Nathalie Akkaoui
Larise Cummings
Jessica Rusby

Wallpaper* Group Editor-in-Chief
Tony Chambers
Publishing Director
Gord Ray
Managing Editor
Jessica Diamond
Acting Managing Editor
Oliver Adamson

Contributor
Paul McCann

Wallpaper* ® is a registered trademark of IPC Media Limited

First published 2006
Revised and updated
2009, 2010, 2011 and 2013

© 2006, 2009, 2010,
2011 and 2013
IPC Media Limited

ISBN 978 0 7148 6459 4

All prices are correct at the time of going to press, but are subject to change.

Printed in China

PHAIDON

Phaidon Press Limited
Regent's Wharf
All Saints Street
London N1 9PA

Phaidon Press Inc
180 Varick Street
New York, NY 10014

Phaidon® is a registered trademark of Phaidon Press Limited

www.phaidon.com

A CIP Catalogue record for this book is available from the British Library.

PHOTOGRAPHERS

LOS ANGELES

A COLOUR-CODED GUIDE TO THE HOT 'HOODS

WEST HOLLYWOOD/MIDTOWN
Home to a raft of happening hotels, restaurants and shops, as well as the vast LACMA

SANTA MONICA/VENICE/CULVER CITY
Hit the beach in Santa Monica, shop in Venice and tour Culver City to see an area on the up

HOLLYWOOD
Avoid the touristy Boulevard and visit the bars and clubs tucked down the backstreets

LOS FELIZ/SILVER LAKE/ECHO PARK
Cool, very cool. Check out the boutiques and cafés as well as the California modernism

BEVERLY HILLS/WESTWOOD
A little staid but still unmissable, thanks to its movie-star glamour and the Getty Center

DOWNTOWN
No longer a no-go zone, Downtown now buzzes with nightlife. MOCA is an LA highlight

For a full description of each neighbourhood, see the Introduction.
Featured venues are colour-coded, according to the district in which they are located.